TEMPERATE FORESTS

SIMON & SCHUSTER
YOUNG BOOKS

First Published in 1992 by
Simon & Schuster Young Books
Campus 400
Maylands Avenue
Hemel Hempstead
Hertfordshire HP2 7EZ
England

British Library Cataloguing in Publication Data

Knapp, Brian
Temperate forests (Caring for environments)
1. Temperate forests – Juvenile literature
I. Title II. Series
574

ISBN 0-7500-1041-X

***Printed and bound** in Hong Kong*

***Author** Dr. Brian Knapp*
***Art Director** Duncan McCrae*
***Illustrator** Mark Franklin*
Designed and produced by
EARTHSCAPE EDITIONS,
86 Peppard Road,
Sonning Common, Reading,
Berkshire, RG4 9RP, UK

Picture credits

t=top b=bottom l=left r=right

All photographs from the Earthscape Editions photographic library except the following: Hutchison Library 28, 29, 34t; Nigel Phillips 22b; ZEFA – 22t, 23, 32t

CONTENTS

8 What are temperate forests?
14 How forests regrow
18 Coniferous forests
24 Deciduous forests
28 Using the trees
38 Is there a future?
44 Glossary
45 Index

1: WHAT ARE TEMPERATE FORESTS?

The world is encircled by two great belts where the climate is favourable to the growth of forests. One girdles the equator and is home to the tropical rainforests. The other, once just as extensive, occurs between the cold lands of the high Arctic and the prairie grasslands. Here two kinds of trees thrive: the deciduous trees like the maple, the oak and the hickory; and the coniferous trees such as the fir, the spruce and the pine.

The deciduous and coniferous trees of these regions share the need to protect themselves against the harshness of winter and the short warm growing season. In this book we shall call them collectively the temperate forests, although other common terms include temperate woodland for the deciduous forest and **boreal** forest for the coniferous forests.

Where have the forests gone?

In these days when people are concerned to protect the tropical rainforest, it is strange to think that people in the industrial countries once had their own rich forest, equally worth preserving and treasuring. But, as today in the poor tropical countries, people who are now prosperous enough to take a balanced view of the natural world were once only too glad to find a use for the temperate forests, as firewood, as hulls for ships and as timber for homes and furniture. They were also glad to see the forests disappear

One of the great spectacles of the deciduous forests *occurs in the Autumn as the leaves begin to turn shades of yellow, red and brown.*

Autumn is called 'Fall' in much of North America because it was one of the most striking sights that the first pioneers beheld who landed in America after their journeys from Europe.

for another reason: a cleared forest was a land that could be used for farming.

The deciduous forests were dealt the harshest blow for they grew in the deep fertile lowland soils near to rivers. These were places where the summers were warm enough and long enough to ripen corn or to provide good pasture for animals. The trees were also hardwoods, trees that grew slowly, putting on a thin sheath of dense, hard wood each year. It is this property of hardness that makes them resistant to attacks by pests whether growing as a tree or when forming the frame of a house, a ship or a barn.

Conifers grow in the colder lands of the north or the higher regions of mountains. Land here was less easy to farm, and conditions much harsher. So fewer people lived in these regions and there were therefore fewer reasons to cut the forests, at least until the railways and the roads made these areas more accessible.

Saved and saved again

The forests of Europe were the first to disappear. To begin with people needed the forests for many things – as grazing grounds for pigs and as places for firewood and building materials. But as the populations grew, so the pressures to cut down more and more forest grew ever stronger. Iron had always been smelted using charcoal made from deciduous trees, and as the industrial revolution gathered pace, so more and more trees were cut.

The last surviving natural forests *lie in the high mountains where they have been difficult to exploit. Here, in the American Rockies, the climate limits the trees to the valleys. The 'tree-line' is very clear. Trees are also absent, however, from the valley bottoms where marshy conditions prevail.*

Many trees survive now only on infertile lands *that are of little use for farming. But such soils can only be home to a small number of acid-tolerant species.*

So great was the demand for timber that at the beginning of the nineteenth century, it was reported that there was not a single living tree standing within 40 kilometres of the naval town of Southampton on the southern English coast.

Although Southampton, with its huge demands from the naval dockyards, may have been an exception, the forests were disappearing fast all over Europe. They were saved from total extinction by the discovery that coal, in the form of coke, could be used to smelt iron. But the forests were still under threat from farmers.

Each country has a different history of deforestation. Great Britain, a small, densely populated country, shows how deforestation can go to extremes. Today it has the smallest percentage of forest of

The world's temperate forest lands

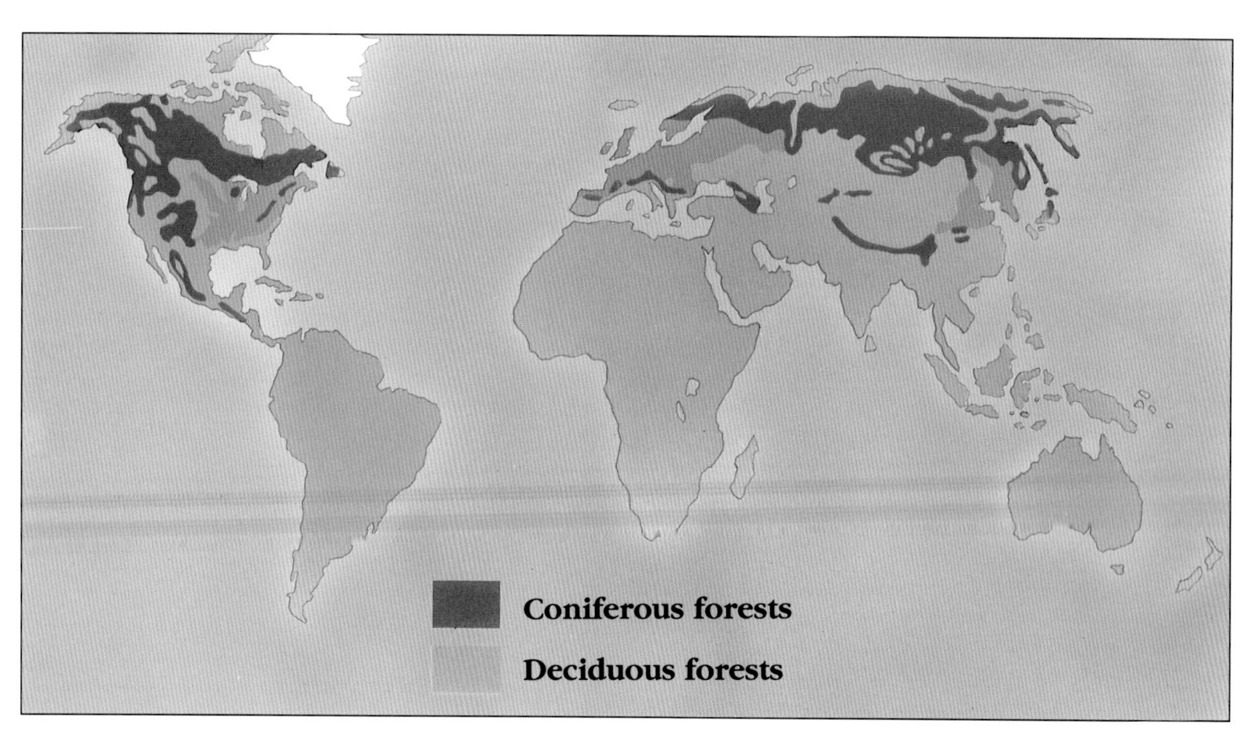

any country in Europe, and Europe in turn has smaller percentages of natural forest left than the Americas.

As people moved off the land to take up new jobs in the towns created by the Industrial Revolution, populations in the towns grew, and as townspeople didn't grow their own food, the pressure on the farms to produce more food steadily increased. In turn this stimulated new

A solitary tree stands *as a reminder of where a hedge used to be. Today the main areas of natural deciduous forest are on the steep slopes of upland valleys where there is little competition from farmland.*

farming methods which in turn required the enlargement of fields and their **enclosure** by walls and fences.

At first the farmers replanted some of the trees lost to farmland along the sides of the fields in rows to make hedges. Today these trees are mature and they can give the impression of a fairly wooded countryside. But in the last 200 years fewer and fewer trees have been planted or replanted. Soon, when the present mature trees die, there will be little to replace them.

Recently the fate of the forests has changed again. The success of farming in developed countries has produced surpluses of food so great that less farmland is required. Today there are plans to replace a small amount of this surplus land with deciduous forests. Just in time.

Conifers get the chop

It is difficult to imagine the deciduous forests as they must have looked 1000 years ago. Legends of Robin Hood and his merry men who lived in the famous Sherwood Forest of central England some 700 years ago could hardly be enacted in the suburbs of the industrial cities that now occupy such sites!

No such changes seem to have happened to the coniferous forests. The area traditionally under coniferous forest remains forested. However, the forests you see today are not the natural ones that used to grow. Rather they are the

A commercial coniferous forest is designed for easy logging. *It has wide treeless avenues called fire breaks to stop the spread of fire, and a balance of species to meet market needs. It is a dark, uninviting place, so unlike a natural coniferous forest.*

Forests provide a pleasant shaded backdrop *for housing estates. But each house that is hidden away in the forests shown in these pictures has been built at the expense of several trees that had to be chopped down to make space.*

The resulting forest is simply a collection of trees; it is not a live forest filled with balanced wildlife. This is not a means of caring for the forest environment, but an unthinking and selfish use of it.

plantations of timber companies which meticulously replant what they have felled – but only with the species that will sell in the marketplace. As a result it is more accurate to think of such lands as being like a wheatfield or a barley field, rather than as a natural environment with a balanced variety of species. The trees are grown so close together that they exclude daylight from the forest floor. It is a technique well suited to creating tall straight tree trunks with few side branches, and therefore few knots in the wood. But it does little for the natural environment.

2: HOW FORESTS REGROW

Small clearings are created *all the time as trees die and fall.*

Caring for an environment means understanding how to help every living thing survive. Any **ecosystem** is a balanced arrangement of many species, both plant and animal. Within the ecosystem each individual, whether it be a massive tree over 50 metres high or the smallest moss, must struggle for survival. This means that the ecosystem is constantly changing, as old members of the forest die back and young ones begin to mature. But the forest ecosystem is also a place with a great ability to fight back against any disaster that might befall it. A major fire or an attack by a pest may be setbacks to a natural forest, but they will never permanently destroy it.

The ability to regrow and adapt to change is the strength of the natural forest and it is the key to understanding how to care for such environments.

Occasionally the forest is entirely destroyed *by a catastrophe. In this case the land was destroyed by the Mount St Helens volcano that erupted in 1980 in Washington state, USA*

The pioneers

A natural forest is not a place that appears neat and tidy. Some trees may lie broken as a result of recent storms, their trunks leaning crazily against others. Others may lie on the ground, their carcasses being attacked by a myriad of insects. In some places trees may be crowding one another out while in other places there is seemingly more than enough room to spare. But this natural environment is not as unorganized as at first it might seem. Each pattern is simply a sign that the forest is constantly renewing itself.

There are many reasons why a forest naturally becomes cleared. A storm might knock over some ancient trees and as they fall these trees may drag down others. The cleared area that results is small. Some people would call it a glade. A fire, caused perhaps by a long dry summer followed by lightning, may burn out a much larger area, leaving only scarred stumps and ash behind. Occasionally something more dramatic may happen, such as when a volcano erupts and levels entire forests.

When a space opens in any natural forest it seems almost impossible for anything to grow up to take its place. Yet, as soon as rain falls or snow melts you will see the first plants, or **pioneers**, sending up their leaves and swiftly coming into bloom with their bright flowers.

The trees take over

The bare open ground is soon colonized by plants which have been blown in from the surrounding forests. Their seeds normally fall in the shade of growing trees where they rot away. However, they get their chance when a space opens and full sunlight shines on the ground. They are

Pioneer plants are soon found flourishing *in the ground that had seemed so bare. This is the forest at Yellowstone, Wyoming, USA, two years after many people had thought the forest was completely destroyed.*

not, of course, the only plants competing for the new ground. Seeds from the trees will be buried in the upper layers of the soil, just waiting for their chance to start growing.

Whereas the pioneers grow very quickly, the tree saplings are much slower at colonizing the open ground. They only grow after the pioneers have provided shade and moisture below their leaves. In this more moist environment the seeds can germinate and the saplings can begin to grow. First they send down deep roots that will nourish the plant as it grows. Only later do they send up stems and branches.

The longer term strategy pays off well, and soon the saplings are racing to compete with each other, shading out the pioneers which then begin to die back. Soon the space has grown over, but only the strongest of the saplings will get enough light to its leaves to become mature; its neighbours will remain stunted and die back. In this way the trees eventually space themselves quite evenly over the reclaimed forest floor.

Many trees begin to develop *by first sending roots down to get water and nourishment from the soil. But before the food in the seed is completely used up the new plants must also make leaves and begin the process of photosynthesis.*

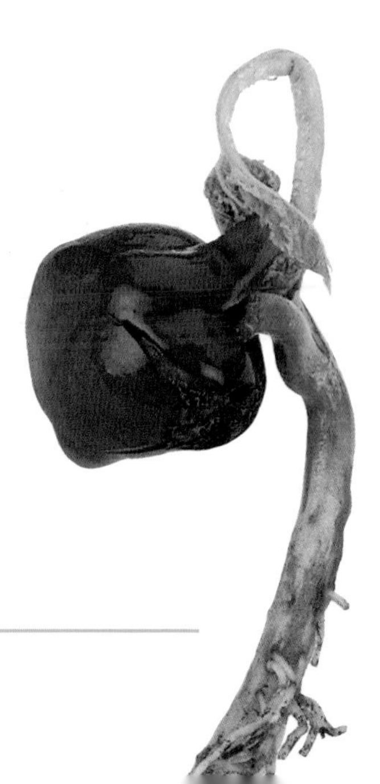

Completing the picture

Even cleared ground can quickly become home for insects and birds. But as time proceeds and the forest begins to regrow, a more varied environment develops which provides shelter and food for more and more species, both large and small.

It will take many decades to complete the regrowth of a mature forest, whether it is deciduous, coniferous or mixed. But even then forests do not stop changing. There is constant competition between each of the species as they continue to jostle for the right to survive. What is vital is that there continue to be young members of each species to replace the ones that die.

Forests are quick to regrow if left alone. *But the most vulnerable stage for a forest is often not when it is growing, but when it is fully grown.*

The forest of coastal Californian redwoods shown in the picture above left is protected from logging, but it is probably too small to be self-sustaining in the longer term.

The mature forest of sycamores and oaks in Yorkshire, England, shown above right, is large enough to regrow, but it is never likely to do so while sheep are allowed to graze, for the sheep will simply eat all the seedlings as they begin to grow.

Both forests are out of long-term balance, but it is not obvious because the present trees are still thriving.

3: CONIFEROUS FORESTS

Because coniferous forests cover both vast areas of cold lowlands and high mountain lands there is much variety to be found. Yet all these forests have many things in common. To begin they are balanced ecosystems. Plants use the sunlight to make leaves and other tissues. These provide the food for the plant-eating animals called herbivores, which, in turn, are food for the meat-eating predators, or carnivores. Eventually all plants and animals die and in their turn are broken down into food for the plants once more by a range of soil life known as decomposers. This is known as the food chain. Together, the balanced, interdependent forms of life and the environment around them make up an **ecosystem**.

Finding a niche

Conifers often grow in harsher environments than deciduous trees. They may be cold, with the ground frosted for months on end, or they may lie under deep blankets of snow. They may also be extremely wet places, where the soil is waterlogged for much of the year. And again, they may even experience long periods of summer drought.

Conifers do not shed all their snow *because it helps to protect the tree from the bitter winter windchill.*

Forests give individual trees much protection. *A **stand** of trees will help create a warmer climate in which they can thrive. It will capture snow that will melt and give moisture for the summer, and the trees will protect each other against strong winds.*

All these harsh conditions have made the conifers very resilient plants, and each group has adapted to a particular environment, or niche. The world probably contains over 500 species of conifer, made up of 45 major groups. The largest group contains the pines, but there is also great diversity in other conifers, such as junipers.

In some cases there are species of conifer that are found only in a particular environment. The best know of these are the redwoods of the California and Oregon coastal fog belt in North America. The world's largest tree, the giant redwood or sequoia, is found only in small parts of the Sierra Nevada mountain range of California and Oregon. The rarest of all, often referred to as a 'living fossil', is the redwood of the Szechuan province of central China.

Most other species of conifers have adapted to cope with a broad range of environments. Nevertheless, they each still clearly have their own territory and there is not a great deal of overlap. Thus, although most forests are dominated by the spruces, firs and pines, the actual species that occur depend closely on the climate. In the dry Rocky Mountains of the USA, for example, ponderosa pine and Douglas fir are the main trees at moderate heights, but lodgepole pine

***Conifers such as pines and redwoods often grow straight and tall**, with few side branches. They leave the forest floor relatively open, and sun can filter down. However, the needles are slow to decompose and they provide little in the way of **nutrients** for other forms of life. As a result few plants grow on the forest floor.*

colonizes wherever the ground has recently been cleared either by fire or lumbering. By contrast, in the wetter lowland regions of Sweden and Finland, as well as in much of Canada, Sitka spruce is the most frequently occurring species.

The survivors

Conifers are able to survive in harsh conditions because they have developed methods of being self-sufficient.

The soils beneath the cold conifer forests are extraordinarily barren of life. Where you might find millions of bacteria swarming over each tiny particle of soil beneath deciduous trees, in the soils of the coniferous forests the bacteria are practically absent because conditions are too cold for them. Bacteria are vital for performing the rapid breakdown of dead tissue, and without them only the much slower acting microscopic plants called fungi can cause decay.

The larger soil animals, such as earthworms, also perform a vital role in soil fertility. They drag dead plant material from the surface and incorporate it in the lower soil layers. In this way they redistribute organic matter more evenly through the soil. However, earthworms do not thrive in wet or cold soils or those where bacteria are absent.

Without earthworms, burrowing mammals such as moles have little to eat and they, too, are absent. As a result there are no animals to loosen or turn over the soil, nothing to drag dead leaves into the soil or to chew it into small pieces ready

Because conifers are evergreens *they shade the forest floor throughout the year. However, as the picture above shows, natural coniferous forests do not completely shade out the ground and a few plants can grow, such as the one shown on the right.*

to be made into **humus**. As a result the soil material simply lies on the surface, and thicker and thicker layers of poorly decomposing plant matter form.

In deciduous forests, trees rely on the soil animals to break down the dead leaves and return the nutrients swiftly to the soil for reuse. Because this doesn't happen in a coniferous forest, the trees cannot expect to use the soil as a major source of food. To cope with this problem the conifers have developed an extraordinary strategy. When they are about to shed any needles, they set in motion a process which sucks as much nutrient from the needle as possible before it eventually drops to the ground.

Dead needles accumulate on the forest floor *because there are few soil animals to drag them into the soil. As water flows through this poorly rotting material it reacts with the leaves and produces an acid. As the acid reaches the mineral soil below, it dissolves, or* ***leaches****, many minerals away. The ash-grey colour of the soil indicates how poor it is.*

This soil is called a ***podzol****, a Russian word from their coniferous forest lands meaning 'ash-coloured soil'.*

***Deer are the main large herbivores** in the temperate forests. Herds may roam over large areas in order to get sufficient food, especially in winter. They cannot survive unless forests have open spaces for ground vegetation to grow and unfenced space for the herds to wander.*

In this way the trees have to look for much smaller supplies of fresh nutrients each year than their deciduous neighbours.

Of course, eventually the leaf litter on the soil surface does break down and releases the few nutrients that it contains. The conifers are expert at scavenging these as well. They send out networks of roots just below the soil surface, ready to catch the nutrients before they are washed though the soil by the spring melt-water or heavy rains.

A special life cycle

Conifers are very adaptable. If the climate is harsh they will grow slowly; if the climate is more kind they will grow faster. Conifers all produce cones containing seeds. Some cones have a special trigger mechanism and will only open and release their seeds when some special conditions exist. In some cases, such as the giant redwood, the cones only open after the heat from a forest fire.

Conifers are softwoods. They grow quickly when they are young and the cells

***Birds find it difficult to gather enough food** in a coniferous forest. This song thrush will have to look far and wide to find sufficient food supply.*

that make their tissues are large. But early growth does not mean that conifers have a short life. Some giant redwoods are over 4000 years old, while the annual growth rings on a bristlecone pine show that some of these trees are over 4900 years! Clearly such ancient trees took a long time to mature and they are not readily replaced once they have been cut down.

Bears still inhabit large areas of forest *in North America, Asia and Europe. They are well equipped to cope with the harsh conditions of a cold winter, but nonetheless, hibernate – a practice common among animals who inhabit the coniferous forests of the world.*

4: DECIDUOUS FORESTS

If you look at a deciduous forest in summer, with the sunshine filtering through the leaves, you might suppose that this was an easy place for all forms of life to find a home. Yet during winter food will be scarce for all animals. It is this change of food supply, more than anything, that decides which creatures can survive in a forest environment.

The broad-leaved trees depend on an abundant supply *of both moisture and nutrients in the soil. Without them they would not be able to grow quickly each spring.*

Wealth in the soil

The secret of good forest growth is in the soil.

When rocks break down in a moist climate they yield a fine material called clay. Clay is important because its surfaces have special properties that allow it to hold on to any nutrients released by plant decay. In effect the clay acts as a kind of bank, trapping the nutrients before they can be washed, or leached, away in the percolating rainwater, but holding them loosely enough so they can be extracted by the plant roots when they are required.

Clays do not produce a fertile soil on their own, however. Clays are naturally sticky and will form into a solid mass that will not let air to the plant roots or let water drain away. In the cooler lands of the coniferous forests, the soil is frozen at depth and the trees keep their roots in the surface. But tree roots penetrate deep into deciduous forest soils in a unique way that keeps the clays separated into clumps, allowing nutrients to be recovered easily from the clays.

Silent web of roots

Clays are not just stores of nutrients. They are also able to soak up water, swelling as they do so. During the winter, therefore, when the trees are not growing, the soil clays absorb water and swell; in the summer, when the demands of the thirsty trees are great, they give up some of their moisture, and shrink slightly. So they are both sources of water and food for the deciduous forest plants. It is this that encourages the tree roots to sink deeply into the soil and to spread out their roots in a huge cone-shaped net.

The roots are not a passive user of the soil. They are also vital for its continued survival because they actively help to break it up. As the roots push down between the clays two things happen. Firstly the roots push the clays aside, loosening the soil and allowing water and air inside. Secondly, through the summer they draw up huge amounts of water, causing the clays to shrink and crack, and thus produce more important cracks and gaps in the soil.

Crucial soil animals

Each year the leaves fall from the deciduous forest trees. But if you go to a deciduous forest you do not sink waist deep in fallen leaves. Look closely and you will find hardly any leaves at all. Unseen, and largely unnoticed, there is a vast army of soil animals at work, dragging the fallen leaves into the soil, chewing them up and turning them into humus.

One of the most important of the soil animals is the earthworm. It is small enough to be able to move about in a soil among the roots of trees without doing damage, but it is big enough to be able to drag leaves underground and, through its burrowings, loosen the soil yet further.

As earthworms move in the upper soil layers, they eat any dead leaf material and digest it, along with any soil material in their path. In their guts are bacteria that break down the plant material and make new substances, including long thread-like gums that bind the soil clays together. As the soil leaves the earthworm, it is no longer simply clay, but a mixture of clay and humus, all intertwined and stuck together. This humus is not only sticky, but also able to soak up water and store nutrients even more effectively than clay.

Soils of the deciduous forests are called *brown earths. They are deep soils, with well mixed mineral and organic matter. The topsoil is usually darkest because here the earthworms have been most active at mixing dead leaves into the soil and producing humus, which is a black colour. Lower down, in the subsoil, the earthworms rarely penetrate and the soil is the lighter brown colour of the weathered rock.*

In their never-ending search for food, earthworms, and other soil creatures, mix over ten tonnes of soil per hectare each year, evenly spreading the soil nutrients on which the trees and other plants depend. Behind them they leave burrows that allow water to seep away after a storm, and they break up the soil into small, stable pieces, or structures. They are the most excellent of gardeners.

Making the most of the seasons

Both plants and animals have to be opportunists. They have to make the most of the spring and summer when the soil is warming and there is enough energy for growth. In the deciduous forest the first to appear are the forest-floor bulbs. Bluebells, crocuses and snowdrops have a bulb from which to draw energy and to give them a head start. They must shoot, put on their leaves, flower and set seed in the small window of opportunity that lies between the end of the cold winter and the arrival of the leaves on the trees.

The deciduous forest floor of spring is garlanded with carpets of white snowdrops, then white and blue crocuses and finally the blue haze of bluebells. Each species takes its turn in using the sunshine, and each has a different growing season to avoid competition. Finally, as spring turns to summer and the leaves on the trees spread their shady crowns, so the bluebells die back and the ferns take over. Meanwhile the bulbs replenish their used food stocks and await the next spring.

In among the branches

There is relatively little deciduous forest life on the forest floor because the tree fruits are high in the branches. Butterflies and other insects find nectar in these high places, as do many birds. Squirrels, too, are adapted to the trees

A deciduous forest in late spring *is typified by a small number of plant species carpeting the floor. Most animals find their food high in the canopy.*

Oak leaf

Shedding leaves is a means of protecting *the tree during the winter, both from the effects of frost and from losing too much moisture by* ***transpiration*** *at a time when the ground may be frozen.*

Cherry leaf

Autumn leaf fall signals the end of the year *for many animals. It is now that they begin to stock up on nuts and berries and prepare for the winter hibernation. The water supply to the leaves is cut off, but the trees do not take much of the nutrients back into the trunks because the earthworms will help to recycle nutrients to the roots for next year.*

to find their food. But there are forest-floor dwellers. Many of the deciduous forest animals are rodents such as the rabbit. Deer move silently through the woods browsing on leaves from trees within their search. They are complemented by foxes and other carnivores to complete the food chain.

The branches of deciduous trees *look stark in winter, but beneath the scaly twigs lie the buds that will quickly burst into flower in spring.*

5: USING THE TREES

Today many people think of forests as a last resort for using land. Forests are slow to grow and hard to harvest. They need large amounts of investment and the return on the money may not be seen for half a century or more. Forests need to be managed with a long-term view, and many people are simply not willing to use their land in this way. As a result, in many countries, forests are grown only on the poorest land and planted with the fastest growing trees, whether or not these are suited to the environment. Only in lands where the numbers of people are small, or the colonization late – Scandinavia, Canada, Tasmania, for example – have substantial natural forests survived.

Peoples of the Siberian forests *are now mostly herders. These people migrate through the forests with their animals, following the age-old paths in search of food.*

But it was not always so. For thousands of years people regarded the forests as a rich source of their needs and many people lived entirely from what the forest could provide. In this way they learned how to live with the forest without destroying it.

The hunter-gatherers

Each of the world's temperate forests had its traditional peoples. For the most part they have long since been absorbed into industrial lifestyles and only traces of their ways and knowledge remain. But many peoples used to live among the natural forests, treating the trees as living things that should be respected and part of the natural order. Some of the Indian tribes of Canada, and those of the mountains of the USA, are examples of such people.

The temperate forests of North America yielded a range of fruits and nuts, from the acorn and pine cone to the hickory nuts and walnuts, together with dozens of varieties of fruits, berries, roots and mushrooms.

But the forest peoples did not have to be vegetarians. A natural forest contains large animals such as the bear and deer together with many small rodents and birds and there are plentiful fish in the streams. Even the onset of winter was not an insuperable problem for people who learned to make storehouses and to preserve their food.

The word totem *comes from the language of the Ojibwa Indians of North America. Many tribes have rich cultures of which the totem pole is a central part. Carved from the trees within the tribal boundaries, they depict animals that have a special relationship with the spirits and way of life of the community.*

If the tribe uses a special animal as the symbol of the totem, then typically the tribe will not eat it, or will have some special reverence towards it. The object of the tribe is therefore to ensure the survival of that particular animal.

Through the use of such symbols and spirit beliefs, many tribes expressed their deep relationship with the natural environment and the need for the long term survival of all the forest's species.

These totem poles are from near Vancouver in British Columbia, Canada.

Above all, the forest people learned how the forest worked, how the animals and plants were part of an ecosystem that needed to stay in balance if it were to survive and provide for their needs. Nowhere is evidence of this respect for the forest clearer than in the many totem poles that the North American tribes constructed for the spirits of their ancestors and their animals.

The onslaught by the farmers

It can be hard to find the wildlife in the denseness of a forest, and as people became more numerous and needed more food it made more sense to domesticate animals rather than to have to hunt them. Domesticated animals need grazing land and this could only be provided by removing the forests.

In Europe the forests were cleared using a technique called slash and burn. Land was first cleared roughly using stone axes, then set on fire. Grasses then colonized the burned land and animals could be grazed. People quickly learned that trees would not grow again on land that was grazed because animals eat the saplings. As a result, it was easy to keep large areas of former forest as open pasture. The information in the table on p. 31 shows how the changes happened in France, a country with natural forests of both deciduous and coniferous species.

Forested landscapes, *such as that shown in the background of the picture below, survive because the steeply sloping land is not suitable for ploughing and because people still use trees for firewood and in other traditional ways.*

Deciduous forests grow in land that is well watered. Their soils are deep and fertile and can be readily adapted to continuous cultivation. But farmers could not eliminate trees entirely for they still depended on them for fuel and building materials. As a result, trees were often replanted in small patches or they were relegated to the boundaries of fields and the most infertile parts of the landscape.

The land brought into farming use was found to be naturally very fertile because trees recycle nutrients in an efficient way, but the land soon loses this fertility if crops are grown year after year. So every few years farmers were obliged to abandon the land they had abused and allow it to grow back as forest, a practice called **fallowing**, or shifting cultivation.

Many countries have suffered a progressive decline in the amount of forest. *These data from France show how the land needed for farming steadily increased over the centuries. The increase in woodland this century has been made possible by improvements in farming methods and government policy to be self-sufficient in forest products.*

Date	Wooded area as a percentage of total land
3000 BC	80
0 AD	50
1400 AD	33
1650 AD	25
1800 AD	15
1900 AD	19
1960 AD	21
1990 AD	24

Modern farming*, such as shown in the picture above, relegates trees to the margins.*

Eventually people developed a rotation between different types of crop, and more recently they have begun using artificial fertilizers to replace the nutrients taken out of the soil by cropping. But none of these techniques are as effective at maintaining soil in good condition as the nature processes associated with forest growth. Ploughing simply disturbs the surface, often compacting the land below. Nothing can loosen the soil the same way as happens in a natural forest. Today the farmland is 'on loan' from the forest. The soil of the temperate forests has a huge capacity for illtreatment before it is fully ruined. In some places farmers have come close to such a state, but erosion of the deep brown soils is still comparatively insignificant. In time this may no longer be the case.

Foresters hold the key

Forestry has always been an important industry in every country with trees. Even today, in many countries homes are still made of wood, even in the suburbs of modern cities. To meet this need, foresters have exploited almost all the world's temperate forests. Caring for the environment has not been a priority in this scheme.

Logging has become highly mechanized *and forests are often clear-cut to allow machines to do much of the hard work and to allow trucks to remove the logs quickly.*

The bigger the trees, the more timber could be gained from each one and the more attractive they become. At first the trees were simply felled and the land discarded. In this way huge areas of forest were destroyed. They were simply

Deciduous forest trees grow more each year than conifers*, although much of the growth will be in the form of branches and leaves, rather than economically useful tree trunk. This type of forest is still being heavily logged. Coniferous forests occupy larger areas and they are being exploited rapidly because the wood is useful for paper and buildings.*

Forest type	**Growth each year** (grams of wood added per square metre of forest)	**Total production** (billions of tonnes)	**World area** (millions square of kilometres)
Deciduous forest	600	4.2	7.0
Coniferous forest	500	6.0	12.0

The world has an enormous appetite for timber. *To suit the machines the aim is often to produce uniform trees of uniform thickness and which all grow to the same height in the same time. This kind of tree farming is not very environmentally sensitive.*

'mining' the trees. When the trees were all cut down the logging companies simply moved their sawmills to a new site.

It took at long time for people even to begin to consider the idea of replanting what had been harvested. The first steps forward were made by the German foresters in the nineteenth century, spurred on by the knowledge that they would soon have no forests left unless they took action.

The theme of stable forest use was taken up most seriously in the USA by the chief of the federal forestry division, Gifford Pinchot, at the beginning of the twentieth century. His view was that

Mechanical logging easily disrupts the topsoil, *leading to erosion during periods of high rainfall.*

forests can provide many products at the same time. Multiple use was not, however, taken seriously either in the USA or in most other countries for many decades. Only in 1960 was a Multiple Use Act passed in the USA to manage the federal forests for 'timber, watershed, range, outdoor recreation, and wildlife and fish purposes'. In many other countries there is still no specific requirement on foresters to look after the heritage of the land at all.

Trees are very bulky and difficult to move. *The cheapest way of transporting them has traditionally been to use rivers as natural floatways. It is for this reason that sawmills tend to be located at the mouths of rivers, especially where they enter lakes that can be used as floating warehouses for the logs. The areas most heavily logged are also those with large rivers, and areas remote from rivers have traditionally been left alone. Only the recent use of large trucks has changed the pattern of logging.*

This table shows the huge increase in demand for paper and board *since 1960. Most paper and board comes from softwood (coniferous forests).*

million tonnes produced	1960	1970	1980	1989
Africa	0.5	0.9	1.7	2.6
North America	43.3	58.4	72.4	87.0
South America	1.5	2.8	5.6	7.9
Asia (incl. USSR)	14.4	25.8	38.3	53.7
Europe	26.2	38.8	50.1	60.4
Oceania	0.9	1.5	2.1	2.3
World	**86.0**	**128.0**	**170.0**	**215.0**

The way people have abused their forests in the past is highlighted by the plight of the giant redwoods in the mountains of California, USA. First seen by people of European descent 200 years ago, these trees were at first too remote to be exploited. But as the population of California grew, so more of the forests were cut down

At this time people did not understand, nor did they concern themselves with the time such trees took to regrow and the special locations to which they were restricted. They simply revelled in the source of timber, regretting not the loss of trees, but the loss of easily obtained timber.

Later, when the area was made a National Park, people still looked at the trees as marvels, and gave little thought to such activities as cutting a hole through the trunk just to get the thrill of driving through the natural arch.

This redwood shows the strain of all the maltreatment. It has been burned away above and its base cut through below. It is now completely dead.

This is a patch-cut forest *showing how vulnerable the soil is to heavy rain after the timber has been cleared. Because so little vegetation is left after logging the natural recycling of nutrients in the soils does not take place and soils get more and more impoverished.*

How foresters treat the land

Even today, the commercial interests of the forests outweigh all other considerations. The Multiple Use Act (see p. 34) does not mention as one of its aims the need to preserve a stable ecosystem. Only in the National Parks of some countries can such aims be carried forward. Foresters still primarily see their role as to provide stands of commercial timber, grown in a way which allows them to harvest it as quickly and cheaply as possible.

'Cheap and quick' has come to mean straight rows and single species. Replanting is now widely practised, but when a balanced system is replaced by a forest of a single species it is not quite what is meant by caring for the forest environment.

As foresters seek to extend the forest land *they look to other poor areas on which to grow their crops. Here a natural* ***wetland*** *has been scored through with straight networks of drains. This will not only destroy the wetland, but it will mean that the sponge effect of the wetland is lost and that, whenever there is a heavy storm, the water will flow more swiftly into rivers and increase the flood hazard.*

The traditional technique of **clear-cutting**, whereby every tree in an area is logged out, is becoming rare. It leaves an open, treeless plot of land that attracts attention because it so obviously despoils the landscape. But the despoliation is not the main reason for changing to a new technique called **patch-cutting**.

Patch-cutting is the removal of patches of trees, leaving other trees all around. It has the benefit of not leaving a large area of soil exposed to erosion, but more importantly, it means that, in any area,

there will be patches of variously aged trees growing. This means that some areas can be logged on a continuous basis. Sawmills and foresters can therefore continue to exploit the same area.

As it happens, the variety of different ages of trees provides some more opportunity for wildlife to flourish, but perhaps the best chance for the temperate forests is the increasing interest being shown by people seeking recreation. The more interest there is in the forest, the more foresters will have to justify, and perhaps amend, their techniques. And they may find ways of harvesting trees that are little more expensive than the present ones, but which are much more environmentally friendly.

This is an area where some 'mother' trees *have been left standing to provide natural regeneration. A more natural spacing of trees is achieved this way, but there are still too few species to provide a natural ecosystem.*

Some trees, such as hazel and willow, *will regrow naturally if cut, or coppiced. This trunk below has been cut clear of the ground and a mass of small shoots can be seen emerging from just below the cut. They can provide a sustainable supply of wood.*

6: IS THERE A FUTURE?

We can only care for our environments if we understand the way they work and appreciate the reasons why they are threatened. Curiously, because the temperate forests have developed in soils that will withstand enormous abuse, most people are unaware of the long term difficulties in store. And people have got used to the lack of trees. Where once they would have relied on local hardwood trees to provide the materials they needed for homes and furniture, today many of the traditional uses have been replaced by brick, steel, concrete, glass and plastic. Where hardwoods are simply the only

Afforestation is not always for the better. *As people have moved out and abandoned their uneconomic farms, so the foresters have often moved in, enlarging their plantations. In future such changes of land use must be accomplished in a much more sympathetic way; they cannot be left to the economics of the machine alone.*

material that will suffice, we find a seemingly inexhaustible supply of timber from overseas (although the destruction of rainforests brings disaster to another environment).

In many industrialized countries, hardwood deciduous trees have been relegated to the position of a decoration. We find tree-lined avenues and tree-spattered parks, and we see trees growing in many gardens. But what we so rarely find is an undisturbed forest.

Recreating a deciduous forest

Because so much of the land that was once deciduous forest has been ploughed up or made into urban areas, it would seem almost impossible to find the great tracts of land that would be needed to make a natural forest again. However, with a little imagination and a willingness to spend a little public money on helping to preserve the natural environment, a lot can still be achieved.

The first example of imagination came as a result of an accident. President Roosevelt of the USA had a hunting lodge in the part of the Appalachian Mountains of eastern USA that had, for centuries, been farmed by subsistence farmers. The farmers were never successful and by the 1930s many had been forced to leave the land. For the first time there was a chance to recreate the forest that had once stood on the spot – a forest which was later to be called Shenandoah National Park.

Out of the misery of the farmers came the opportunity to begin a process of buying up land to make a whole forest. It was not an easy job, and it still covers only a single ridge some 70 kilometres long. But with careful management by the National Park Service, the park is thriving. What is more, by being a National Park, it has also been possible for Shenandoah to attract people who, as they hike the trails or follow the nature walks, begin to understand a little more about the complexity of the natural world that is worth preserving.

Making use of abandoned land

Recently the opportunity has arisen to create more forest by using land that has been abandoned after quarrying or some other industrial activity. Many such areas

Tourists demand an interesting environment to walk in. *The growth of nature trails encourages people to become more aware of the forest ecosystem.*

of land are near to towns and cities and so reforesting such areas gives city people a taste of the countryside on their doorstep. So, starting with abandoned industrial sites such as gravel workings and old coal sites, local governments and charitable bodies have begun patiently to create 'Country Parks'– lands where people are given free access for recreation, but where the theme is conservation. They are designed and run on ecosystem principles, but with a difference that points the way forward to more ways of recreating our natural forests.

A new forest in the making: *this is a corner of a Country Park.*

Each country park focuses on accessibility. One site is chosen and a car park, information office and other facilities provided. This acts as a 'honey-pot', a place which attracts all the people who would visit the park. Next, it is recognized that many people want to have outdoor recreational facilities such as golfing and sailing, so these are placed near the car park. The result is to focus the most popular uses in one part of the park. This leaves the rest of the park for the more adventurous and those who seek a quieter way of passing the time.

One area may focus on angling, another on simply bird watching, a third merely provides rambling paths. As a result, people always find they can do what they want to do, but by careful design the park also provides areas that are very difficult to get to, and therefore places where the natural environment can start to regain a foothold. With careful replanting, such places can begin the long process of recovery, and in time they will become balanced, even if small, forests.

The legacy of overfarming

In a world that is short of food, it seems unbelievable that some places grow too much food. But this is the case in many industrial countries. Farming has simply become so efficient that all the requirements for food can be met from smaller and smaller areas of land. This gives a unique chance to recreate forests in areas where there is little public pressure. Land can now be set aside from farming and replanted with forests, and all with some government subsidies. Here, then, is an opportunity to add to the forest cover on a bigger scale than would ever be possible in the Country or National Parks. It is a chance to use the trees to help to absorb carbon dioxide and dust and to make the environment cleaner and more diverse.

There is nothing wrong with people living in *an area that is actively managed for timber. The presence of people will increase public awareness about the problems of maintaining an ecosystem and it should result in a better balance of species and tree spacing. But it will be a process of give and take. The residents cannot expect to live in a fossilized world of mature trees. That would not be natural either.*

Learning to live without plantations

Timber is still a major resource. Today there is no prospect of countries removing the coniferous forests in the way that they cleared the deciduous forests. In this respect, at least, the forests are safe. Indeed, there are massive replanting schemes underway on land that had once been cleared of forest for upland grazing. But simply having a forest of trees is not enough. It has to be a balanced forest, a place where the timber that needs to be

There is much land that can be brought into use. *Old mine workings are an ideal site for afforestation or mixed use.*

The greatest threat to the temperate forests today *is neither the saw mill owner nor the farmer, but every one of us who wants to drive a motor car or use electricity freely. These trees are dying from the effects of acid rain. It is a clear example of how each one of us is responsible for the global environment, we cannot shrug it off as someone else's problem.*

taken can be removed and yet the land preserved in a more balanced way.

In the end, the changes in forestry practices that provide for more natural growth will be influenced by the views of the general public. For decades there has been an outcry against replanting logged areas with straight rows of identical trees. In the last few years foresters have responded to this by planting screening trees around the **plantations**, and by trying to make plantations of several species, arranged along the contours of the ground rather than in grid-iron patterns. But such changes are simply superficial. Caring for the coniferous forest environment needs much more than that. In essence the nature of forestry has not changed, and it is still geared to logging out by large tree-chewing machines. Caring for the environment means finding ways of making the machines adapt to the environment, not straightjacketing the environment to the needs of the machine. There is still much to be done on this front.

The scourge of acid rain

In this book we have explained how the temperate forest environments work and how they have been under the obvious threat of farmers, sawmill owners and the spread of towns and cities. It is easy to see the effects of these groups. But today, there is something happening to all the temperate forests that cannot be easily explained by the action of the woodman or the farmer. It is something that is killing off the natural forests as well as plantations; it is something that cannot be smelled or seen; and it is more effective than any natural pest. It is the pollution created by our modern way of life: the sulphur dioxide that is sent into the air in hundreds of millions of tonnes each year, and which, when mixed with raindrops in clouds causes the scourge of the temperate forests. It is **acid rain**.

Acid rain is often created by the pollution of one country and kills the trees of another that happens to be downwind of the pollution. The trees of southern Canada are being killed by the acid rain created in northern USA; the trees of Germany are being killed by the pollution of Czechoslovakia; and the trees of southern Norway and Sweden are being killed by the pollution from most of western Europe.

Acid rain is especially lethal in areas with coniferous forest. The soils of these places are already acid, and further acidity from acid rain causes stress in the trees that they simply cannot handle. Acid rain dissolves the aluminium that is in the soil which is normally in a form not able to be absorbed by the tree roots. When aluminium is released it poisons the trees. Extra ozone gas produced by motor cars places yet further stress on the trees ability to breathe. Today, thousands of square kilometres of coniferous forests are quietly dying. It is a tragedy for which all the country parks and national parks cannot compensate.

Trees are easiest to preserve *when there is an economic reason for their existence. The forest clothing the top of this hill is helping to absorb the rainwater and prevent it flooding the valleys downstream where many people live. It is far cheaper, and far more economically sensible, to plant trees than to build dams and create land-flooding reservoirs.*

Because these trees serve a flood-prevention role, they can be grown in a more balanced and natural way than if they were needed solely for timber. The mature plantation seen in the background of this picture was planted long before such ideas became widespread.

GLOSSARY

acid rain
rain which contains gases of sulphur and nitrogen and which make the rain into a weak acid. These gases are mostly produced as pollution

boreal
the name given to describe the cool moist zone that is occupied by the majority of coniferous forests. It lies between the cold tundra and the warmed deciduous woodland zones

brown earth
the name of a deep, fertile soil that forms under deciduous forests. It has a dark brown surface layer consisting of a mixture of mineral particles and decayed plant matter

clear-cutting
the method of forestry whereby all the trees in a forest are felled and the land completely cleared. New saplings are then planted, but the forest will not be able to be harvested again for many years

ecosystem
a balanced arrangement of plants, animals, soil and climate. An ecosystem is a stable unit, with the decay of dead organisms providing the food for those that are growing

enclosure
the method of dividing up land by means of fences, hedges or walls. It was a system invented to make it easier to supervise animals

fallow
the process of leaving a plot of land uncultivated for a number of years so the natural ecosystem can begin to rebuild and store nutrients back in the soil

humus
the decomposed remains of dead organisms. Humus is a black material made of particles the same size as clay

leaching
the process of dissolving and carrying away the nutrients that would otherwise be available in a soil for plant use

nutrients
the chemical foodstuffs that plants use to grow new tissue. Tree nutrients include nitrogen, phosphorous, potassium and calcium

patch-cut
the method of cutting patches of forest and leaving neighbouring patches undisturbed. This provides a way of getting an annual harvest from a forest

photosynthesis
the process by which sunlight is used as the energy source to make new plant growth. Photosynthesis is the basis of almost all the food chains on earth

pioneers
the first species to grow again in a region that has been cleared. Most pioneers grow from seed and are annuals

plantation
a type of forest where trees are managed and harvested rather than allowed to grow in natural patterns

podzol
the name for a soil where the climate is cool and wet. The topsoil consists of unmixed layers. Podzols are known for their acidity and low fertility

stand
the name given to a group of trees of the same species that occur together within a forest

INDEX

abuse 38
acid rain 43, 44
afforestation 38
animals 27
Arctic 8
ash 15

bacteria 20
boreal 8, 44
branches 16
brown earth 25, 44
building 10
burrowing 21

carbon dioxide 41
carnivores 18, 27
clay 24
clear-cutting 36, 44
climate 20
cones 23
conifer 8, 18
conservation 40
Country Parks 40
cropping 32

deciduous 8, 18, 24
decomposers 18, 20
deforestation 11

earthworm 21, 25
ecosystem 14, 18, 29, 36, 40, 44
enclosure 12, 44
erosion 32

fallow 32, 44
farmers 11, 39
farming 9, 40
fertile 30
fertilizer 32
fire 15, 20
firewood 10
flood 36, 43
fog 19
food 12
food chain 18
forestry 33
fuel 30
fungi 20

giant redwoods 35
glade 15
growth rings 23

hardwood 9, 38
hedges 12
herbivores 18, 22
heritage 34
hibernation 23, 27
housing 13
humus 21, 25, 44

iron 10

leach 21, 24, 44
leaf litter 22
logging 36, 42

mountain 18

National Parks 36, 35, 39
needles 20, 22
niche 19
nutrients 20, 22, 24, 44

organic matter 20
ozone 43

patch-cutting 36, 44
photosynthesis 16, 44
pioneers 14, 44
plantation 42, 43, 44
ploughing 32
podzol 21, 44
pollution 43

range 34
recreation 37, 40
redwood 19
replanting 36, 40
reservoirs 43
roots 16, 22
rotation 32

sawmills 33, 37, 42
screening trees 42
season 26
seeds 16, 23
shifting cultivation 32
slash and burn 30
soil 20
species 14
stand 19, 36, 44
stems 16
storm 15
subsidies 40
subsistence 39
sunlight 15

timber 9, 12, 33, 35, 39
topsoil 25
totem pole 29
traditional people 28

volcano 14, 15

watershed 34
wetland 36
wildlife 34, 37
winter 24